Grandfather Kashy Koala

The Journey

Margaret Kamla Kumar
Laila Savolainen

Copyright © 2022
The moral right of Margaret Kamla Kumar to be identified as the Author and Laila Savolainen as the Illustrator of the work has been asserted by them in accordance with the Copyright, Designs and Patents Act 1988.

All rights reserved. No part of this book may be used or reproduced, stored in a retrieval system, or transmitted in any form, or by any means electronic, mechanical, recording, photocopying, or in any manner whatsoever without permission in writing from the publisher, except for the inclusion of brief quotations in a review.

A catalogue record for this book is available from the National Library of Australia

ISBN: 978-0-6454789-4-5 (hardback)
ISBN: 978-0-6454789-0-7 (paperback)
ISBN: 978-0-6454789-1-4 (ebook)

Author: Margaret Kamla Kumar
Illustrator: Laila Savolainen

Interior and Cover Layout: Pickawoowoo Author Services
Print and Channel Distribution: Lightning Source / Ingram (US/UK/AUS/EUR)

Publisher: Uma Publishing Group
www.umapublishing.com

Dedication

This book is dedicated to protecting and sustaining the flora and fauna of the environment.

Grandfather Kashy Koala sat high up on the top branches of a gum tree.

From time to time, he would look out over the plains from the Brisbane Ranges, and he would wonder. Sometimes, he would close his eyes to think. Other times he would bury his head in his chest to smell his fur. A few times, he would scratch and pull at his fur to see how quickly they dropped from his skin.

All these actions made him reflect on how quickly time was passing. He knew he had to act without delay if he wanted his koala family to be healthy and well. Time was of the utmost importance here.

Grandfather Kashy Koala began to think long and hard. Should he warn the others? After all, he was much older. He had his experiences.

All they had was their friskiness and their little grunts, screams and sounds of approval or delight. He looked over to where the little koalas were playing, jumping and chasing each other from branch to branch.

The sun was high in the sky when Grandfather called out to a little koala. "Come here, Koalakin," he said, using his favourite nickname for the little one.

Koalakin clambered over some branches and came and stood by Grandfather's knee, quietly.

He knew when Grandfather Kashy was serious.

"Your coat is too thin," Grandfather Kashy said pinching him. He looked piercingly at Koalakin.

His nose quivered. "Tell your mother to feed you more gum leaves. The winter will be very cold. You must move out into the thicker bush to eat more leaves to make your fur thick."

"But Grandfather, there are hardly any bushes and forests around. Mother complains that you cannot see the trees for the houses."

"Use your nose, Koalakin. We all can smell deeply. Use your nose! Twitch it around! That is why you have it! Smell the air! Can't you smell the gum leaves? Where there is a smell of gum leaves, the land is your friend. That is when you move in that direction. Enough! Run along now and tell your mother."

Koalakin shimmied down a few branches, in haste, to where his mother was sitting. She was cleaning out her fur, picking out seeds and twigs, one by one. "Mother, Grandfather says we have to move from here. He says I am too thin."

Hearing this, Mama Akashi Koala snorted in the way koalas do. "Ha," she said. "Grandfather and his ideas! As usual, he will make sage-like comments. Go and play."

She went back to cleaning her fur.

The sun had begun to go down when Mama Akashi Koala finished cleaning herself. She looked around. All the other koalas were preparing to leave. "Perhaps, Grandfather is right," she thought to herself. "I should do the same."

So, she gathered herself up, latched Koalakin onto herself and began to follow her mates.

Mama Akashi Koala and her mates began to move from branch to branch with Grandfather Kashy Koala leading the way. The journey was slow.

They had never moved from their territory before and had to watch where they were going. They also had never travelled long distances, so had to take a number of rests, in between.

Also, it was safer to move between dusk and dawn.

In some of these areas, there were only houses. They had to cross areas on foot as there was not a tree to be seen.

In another area, the trees had all been burnt down because there had been some big fires. They saw a number of their kith and kin lying still. There were a few that were moving very slowly.

Koalakin stopped and stared at them wondering what had happened.

Mama Akashi Koala shaded his eyes in her fur and hurried him along. She also did not want him getting lost.

The journey to their new home, where they could find more gum leaves was slow and tiring. On some days, there were hardly any trees to gather food.

They clambered along some dried riverbanks and skirted around some wattle shrubs and clumps of grass.

It was tiring work for Koalakin, but he kept on going. He trudged after Mama Akashi Koala. He sensed that Grandfather Kashy knew what he was doing and that was that.

Grandfather was taking them to a better place.

After what seemed like so many moons and so many stars, Grandfather Kashy's nose began to quiver. He could smell gum leaves!

Grandfather Kashy sensed that his nose was sending him a message about food!

It was telling him that if they kept going straight and then turned southwards, they would come to a coastline.

Grandfather Kashy did just that. All the koalas in the group began to do that too.

Following Kashy Koala, they began to climb up the few trees that were there.

At long last, Grandfather Kashy led them to where the forest met the sea. From the particular quiver in his nose, Grandfather Kashy could tell that they had moved in the right direction.

It was a land area that they had not seen before. All the other koalas' noses began to quiver too.

They saw that they were in an area that had many forests. There was also a river surrounding the trees.

And then there was the sea!

Grandfather Kashy Koala called out, "We shall stop here."

Mama Akashi Koala and her koala mates looked around. They were very happy with their new place. There were no houses around. All they saw were varieties of gum trees lined up one by one in one forest and another and another! Each one had lush green leaves!

Koalakin and his friends lost no time in scampering up and down the trees eating the delicious leaves. This was the food they needed!

Each koala family claimed a tree as their own.

Grandfather Kashy Koala sat on the tallest tree stretching out his tired paws and limbs. He held a leaf and smelt it. It was the perfect variety. He smiled and began munching the leaf, all the while sunning himself, in the early morning sun.

Forthcoming Titles

www.ingramcontent.com/pod-product-compliance
Lightning Source LLC
Chambersburg PA
CBHW061135010526
44107CB00068B/2952